Feel the Beat!

Dancing in Music Videos

Jenai Cutcher

rosen central™

The Rosen Publishing Group, Inc., New York

Special thanks to Maria DiDia

Published in 2004 by The Rosen Publishing Group, Inc.
29 East 21st Street, New York, NY 10010

Library of Congress Cataloging-in-Publication Data

Cutcher, Jenai.
    Feel the beat! : dancing in music videos / Jenai Cutcher.
    p. cm. — (The curtain call library of dance)
    Summary: Discusses dance in music videos, providing some vocational
    guidance for prospective dancers.
    Includes bibliographical references and index.
    ISBN 0-8239-4558-8 (lib. bdg.)
    1. Dance—Juvenile literature. 2. Music videos—Juvenile literature.
    [1. Dance. 2. Music videos. 3. Dance—Vocational guidance. 4. Vocational
    guidance.] I. Title. II. Series.

GV1596.5.C88 2004
792.8—dc22
                                                              2003015368

Manufactured in the United States of America

CONTENTS

INTRODUCTION

The set is a playground of flashing lights, raised platforms, and high-tech equipment. Hair and makeup artists are skirting through the cast of dancers, making last minute adjustments. Production people move about, positioning large bright lights and cameras. You stand on your mark, waiting patiently as the director and choreographer discuss the next series of shots. To stay ready and keep your nerves under control, you run through your dance moves in your head. At the same time, you do some stretching to keep your muscles warm and loose. The star, America's hottest new pop idol, then walks onto the set. As she walks by, she gives you a quick smile. She takes her place in the front of you and the other dancers. The music starts. The director yells, "Action!" You begin the choreography. Your case of nerves disappears as you execute each dance step perfectly. You're flushed with excitement and energy as the camera turns toward you.

You're doing what you've trained so hard for—dancing your way through your first music video!

● Many pop stars, such as Janet Jackson, rely on music videos to get their music out to the fans. Music videos often feature dynamic footwork and pulsing music to stir the audience's emotions.

CHAPTER I

MUSIC VIDEO HISTORY

Dance in Movies and Television

Music and dance have always been art forms that work together. Each one has been influencing the other for centuries. However, since the invention of movies and television, music and dance have been changing at a rapid pace.

Movie and TV producers quickly learned that presenting music and dance in movies and television would be very successful. Movies that featured singing and dancing were called musicals. In musicals, characters use song and dance to further the movie's story. Some of the most famous American-made movie musicals include *The Wizard of Oz*

(1939), *Singin' in the Rain* (1952), *West Side Story* (1961), and *Grease* (1978).

In the early days of television, variety shows that copied the style of vaudeville productions were very popular. Vaudeville shows were entertainment which offered a variety of acts. Many TV variety shows featured a chorus of dancers performing big production numbers. For example, *The Jackie Gleason Show* was famous as the TV home of the June Taylor Dancers.

Rock and Roll

Rock and roll music developed in the 1950s. Its popularity swept the country and

affected the kinds of movies and TV shows that were made. Up to this time, the movie musicals and TV shows that were being produced were aimed at adults. However, movies and TV shows began to be aimed at teenagers. One of the first rock and roll performers to be featured in a movie musical was Elvis Presley. Presley

● Since its release in 1939, *The Wizard of Oz* has become a beloved family movie classic. Shown are (from left to right): Bert Lahr (the Cowardly Lion), Ray Bolger (the Scarecrow), Judy Garland (Dorothy Gale), and Jack Haley (the Tin Man). The actors displayed their dancing skills as they danced over the yellow brick road on their way to see the Wizard.

starred in such films as *Jailhouse Rock* (1957). The movie featured many song and dance numbers set against stunning movie sets.

America Dances

In 1957, Dick Clark brought popular radio songs and performers to television with *American Bandstand.* *Bandstand* featured teenagers dancing to the latest in pop music. Viewers were able to learn the latest dance crazes from performers' appearances, such as Chubby Checker doing his hit song and dance, "The Twist." *Soul Train*, another show that included young people dancing, featured the music of Motown that was so popular in the 1970s.

The Beginnings of Music Videos

In the early 1960s, The Beatles and their music swept the world. Fans went crazy for the Fab Four. The Beatles' first movie, *A Hard Day's Night*, was a huge hit. It introduced film techniques, such

The Ed Sullivan Show

The Ed Sullivan Show was one of the most popular and influential of all TV variety shows. It ran from 1948 until 1975. Many famous pop stars including Marvin Gaye, the Rolling Stones, and The Beatles performed on this show. Ballerina Margot Fonteyn, tap dancer Peg Leg Bates, and the June Taylor Dancers also made appearances. Peter Gennaro was the resident choreographer in the show's later years and brought dance on television to a whole new level.

as quick edits and slow motion, that would later be used in modern music videos.

Another popular rock group of the 1960s was The Monkees. The group had its own weekly TV show that featured the band performing its songs. The story would

● The Beatles set the music world on its ear with their clever and timeless songs. The group also experimented with making short films set to their music. They made two feature movies, *A Hard Day's Night* (1964) and *Help!* (1965), as well as numerous TV appearances.

sometimes be stopped for a music video–like interlude.

As popular as these TV

shows were, they were no match for the new generation of music video shows introduced with the creation of MTV in the early 1980s. *American Bandstand* was cancelled in 1989. *Soul Train*, although still on the air, no longer reaches as wide an audience as it once had.

● *Soul Train* started as a local weekly dance show seen in Chicago, Illinois, in 1970. By October 1971, it was seen by a national audience. The series became a showcase for the brightest talents in rhythm and blues, hip-hop, gospel, and jazz. Pop stars such as Elton John, seen here in a 1970s appearance, have also performed on the show.

CHAPTER 2
MUSIC VIDEO DANCERS

The Creation of MTV

Michael Nesmith, once a member of The Monkees, came up with the idea for a TV show that would air videos of popular music performers. He sold the idea, called Popclips, to a company named Warner Amex. This company used Popclips as the basis for creating the MTV Network.

MTV, or Music Television, debuted on August 1, 1981, on cable television. This new outlet for the music industry gave recording stars a visually powerful way to promote their music. MTV's style of hard-hitting music, dazzling visuals, and quick editing helped attract millions of new fans to pop music.

From their beginning, music videos featured dancing that grabbed and held the viewer's attention. Some pop stars of the 1980s were also talented dancers. Pat Benatar danced in some of her videos. Toni Basil, a singer and choreographer, danced along with cheerleaders in her hit music video, "Mickey." In his videos, Prince performed quick dance solos that included turns and jumping down into splits. Michael Jackson featured fancy footwork in all his videos, such as "Billy Jean" and "Beat It." Madonna used her training as a modern

● The five original MTV VJs, or video jockeys, began a new breed of TV star. They were (from left to right): Mark Goodman, Martha Quinn, J. J. Jackson. Alan Hunter (crouching), and Nina Blackwood.

dancer to good use as she danced up a storm in such music videos as "Material Girl" and "Dress You Up." "Material Girl" was nominated in 1985 for a MTV Music Video Award for Best Choreography in a Video.

Michael Jackson changed dance on MTV forever with his landmark video, "Thriller." Jazz, hip-hop, breakdancing, and large groups, performing tight, precise choreography, were all-important elements in "Thriller" and other Jackson videos. He used dance as a new way to tell the stories of the songs he sang. Dance students all over the world wanted to learn how to move like Michael.

Other artists followed Jackson's lead and created videos in which dance and choreography took center stage. Among them were Michael's sister, Janet Jackson, MC Hammer, Paula Abdul, Madonna, Britney Spears, 'N Sync, and Jennifer Lopez. Not

Fun Fact

Toni Basil worked as a choreographer on two popular 1960s TV dance shows— Hullabaloo *and* Shindig. *In the early 1980s, she codirected several music videos. In recent years, Basil choreographed the movies* Legally Blonde *(2001) and* Sunset Strip *(2000).*

only were these performers great dancers, but their videos featured some of the best backup dancers performing in music videos. The dancers performed choreography by top professionals in the business, such as TJ Espinoza and Tina Landon.

TJ Espinoza

TJ Espinoza has performed with Christina Aguilera, Gwen Stefani, and Gloria Estefan. He is best known,

however, as Britney Spears's favorite dancer. Espinoza performed with Spears for two years. He danced with her on concert tours, TV appearances, and in music videos. He was a featured dancer in six Britney Spears videos including, "...Baby One More Time" and "Oops!... I Did It Again."

Espinoza began taking gymnastics in San Jose, California when he was thirteen years old. He also studied jazz and ballet, as well as African and salsa dancing. He is working on a solo singing career and recently began recording an album.

● Britney Spears got her start as a member of *The Mickey Mouse Club* at the age of eleven. However, she burst onto the pop music scene with her debut album, *... Baby, One More Time*, in 1998. She quickly caught people's attention with energizing dance routines in her TV videos.

15

Tina Landon

Tina Landon is a veteran dancer and choreographer. She began her career as a Los Angeles Lakers cheerleader, as had Paula Abdul. Landon's big break came when she landed a main dancing role in Michael Jackson's "Smooth Criminal" video. Later, when Abdul was casting dancers for Janet Jackson's "What Have You Done for Me Lately?" she called on Landon. This began a long working relationship with Janet. While performing in Janet's Rhythm Nation tour, Landon began coaching Janet informally on her choreography and performance. This led to Landon's career as a video choreographer videos.

Her choreography for Michael and Janet Jackson's "Scream" and Ricky Martin's "Livin' la Vida Loca" earned her MTV awards. Today's hottest dancers, like Shawnette Heard and Marty Kudelka, now look to Tina Landon for inspiration.

● Tina Landon has won many awards for her choreography. She is also a five-time MTV Choreography Award Nominee and a two-time Bob Fosse Award Nominee.

Shooting a Music Video

While it can be lots of fun, shooting a music video also takes lots of hard work. Each video shoot is different than any other. They vary, depending on the artist, style of music, location, budget, concept, and other factors—both artistic and practical. For example, there may be dancing in only a few short segments of the video or throughout the entire song. Sometimes dancers might have to perform the choreography with a large group. Other times they may be asked to freestyle alone.

Large-scale dance videos take the most time and money to make. Dancer Shawnette Heard reported that Janet Jackson's "All for You" video had 17-hour shoot days! On the other hand, only one other dancer appeared with Scottie Gage in "I Never Knew" by Gloria Gaynor. Their dancing took only a few short days to shoot.

Dancing Live and Dancing in Music Videos

Dancing in a music video is a very different experience than dancing onstage. In a live show, performances flow continuously. In music video dancing, the performance is filmed and then edited.

Replacing a live audience with a film camera changes the approach to the choreography and performance. Overall, the filming process happens much more quickly. Because costs are very high, production companies move quickly. Casting dancers, rehearsing, and shooting a music video may take only a few days. Often, the final version is the result of editing. What you see on television may be very different than what was first performed.

One of the biggest challenges for video dancers is "staying in frame." Because a director may want certain camera shots, dancers have to be careful to perform all their moves within a small amount of space. Otherwise, they could be cut out of the camera's picture, or frame.

Being on the Set

There is a lot of "hurry up and wait" during the making of music videos. This stop-and-go action is necessary because it takes time to set up a scene so it can be filmed. Equipment, props, sets, and performers have to be in the right place. You could find yourself standing around for hours in your costume, waiting for action to be called. The specific action is then shot in a matter of seconds. The action is often repeated several times and filmed from different camera angles. This allows the final edited video to show the same action from different perspectives. The editing process adds lots of interest and excitement to the filmed performance. For example, you may be filmed doing very quick dance moves. However, once the director is in the editing room, he or she might decide to show some or all of your

● Performers in music videos need to know how to hit their marks. A mark is a spot on the ground that a dancer or a singer has to step on to make sure he or she will be in the camera's frame.

moves in slow motion. He or she might even decide that some or all of the video appear only in one color or in black and white. Other special effects are often added. You might even find yourself glowing in the dark in the final video, thanks to special effects!

Another thing to realize about shooting a music video is that you may never even get to dance with the star. Depending on schedules and other factors, sometimes the music star does his or her work after all the other filming for the video has been done.

Dancing for a Reason

Dance in movies and musical theater is part of the production and supports or advances the story. Dance in music videos is very different because it usually supports the song or story, and spotlights the recording artist. For example, in Michael Jackson's "Beat It" video, two groups of dancers played two different warring gangs. Their dance moves were used to convey the tension between the two sides. Jackson's role as the hero was defined by the way he resolved the situation with his amazing footwork.

● Michael Jackson, seen here on the set of his video, "Billy Jean," is credited with helping to popularize dance in music videos.

CHAPTER 3
CAN I BE AN MTV DANCER?

What It Takes To Be a Music Video Dancer

There's no question that the more versatile you are as a performer, the better your chances of getting "cast," or selected to perform, in music videos. From rock and pop to rap and hip-hop, dance styles change with each type of music.

Jazz Dance

The most important training to have for music video dance is traditional jazz technique. Traditional jazz refers to the specific technical approaches of teachers like Gus Giordano, Luigi, and Frank Hatchett. Traditional jazz technique is highly stylized. There are correct and incorrect ways to execute moves. Most large group choreography in music videos is based on jazz. In this style of dance, one of the goals is to get all the dancers to look the same when they are dancing in unison.

Hip-Hop

Equally present in music video dance is hip-hop and all its subcategories: break-dancing, popping and locking, freestyling, and more. Classes in these styles are often taught by dancers and choreographers who work in the music video field. By studying with them, you are not only learning the combinations currently seen on

● Hip-hop has become more than just a musical trend. It has changed the way people dress and talk. Its influence can also be found in movies and television.

MTV and VH1, but also giving these professionals a chance to see you.

Ballet

Your training in jazz and hip-hop should be supplemented with a strong foundation in ballet. Ballet class is the place to work on your alignment, strength, and flexibility. Exercises at the barre, in the center, and across the floor are all designed to condition your muscles and improve your technique in specific ways. Even if ballet is not your favorite way to dance, it should always remain part of your dance study.

If you are a beginner, ballet class is also a good opportunity to develop your dance vocabulary. Most choreographers rely on some ballet terms to communicate their move-

ment to dancers. Knowing ballet vocabulary can make you a faster learner, thus a better dancer.

Tap

Theatrical tap dancing is not often used in music videos, but even if you are not asked to perform it, studying tap—especially rhythm tap—can develop both your musical and move-

● Gregory Hines (below) was considered one of the greatest tap dancers of his generation. Hines was also a movie actor, starring in *White Nights* (1985) with ballet dancer Mikhail Baryshnikov. Hines also appeared in *Tap* (1989) with tap dancing greats Sammy Davis Jr. and Savion Glover.

● Justin Timberlake (on right in photo) got his start in the 1990s as one of the members of the pop group 'N Sync. Timberlake has sung and danced his way into his own solo career. Many people have compared his dance style to Michael Jackson's.

ment skills. Understanding the meter, tempo, and structure of a song all comes with tap training.

Freestyling and Improvisation

Many videos, especially for rap music, call on the dancers to freestyle, or improvise. When you improvise, you don't have to worry so much about remembering choreography or staying together with the other dancers. However, you do need to be able to create impressive movement phrases that express your individuality and reflect the tone of the music at the same time. Improvising is a skill that must be learned and practiced, like any other.

Other Important Skills

Casting directors and agents will often ask for "tricks" at the end of an audition. The ability to do a back flip or spin a basketball might get you a job. Being able to speak a language other than English or even the ability to make crazy facial expressions might come in handy!

25

Being a Triple Threat

Some music videos seem like mini-movies that bring a story to life. In this case, the director may be looking for characters, not simply dancing bodies, to back up the star. Acting is something you can study, just like dance—through classes, workshops, and experience. Studying singing is also a good way to learn how to interpret song lyrics. In the entertainment business, a performer who can dance, sing, and act is called a triple threat. People who are triple threats are usually placed toward the top of the casting lists.

Be Prepared for Anything

With technical standards constantly rising, you can also expect the choreography to

Los Angeles or New York?

New York City is home to many dancers and music video shoots. However, many people in the industry feel that Los Angeles is the place to be if you are serious about being a music video dancer. Los Angeles is home to the major agents who handle music video dancers. More auditions for music videos are held in Los Angeles. If you do decide to move, you will have to weigh the pros and cons of both cities. For instance, apartments in New York are very expensive. However, in Los Angeles, you will need to have a car to get around. Any decision you make should be thought out carefully and discussed with your parents.

be increasingly hard. Much of what you see in music video dance today is very fast, sharp, and precise execution of difficult moves. You will never know exactly what you will be asked to do as a music video dancer—that's part of the excitement. You can be sure, though, that it will take a lot of hard work and discipline to succeed. Remember that most jobs you go for will be as a "backup dancer." This means you will literally be in the background, supporting the singer and the main dancers. As a backup dancer, you need to be well prepared and a be team player.

As your knowledge and capabilities increase, so will your job prospects. The more things you can do well, the more roles you can consider. However, training is also a juggling act. You only have so much time and money to spend on classes. Decide what you want to focus on and what skills will be most valuable to you for the music videos you want to be in.

● Los Angeles has become the place to be for aspiring music video dancers.

CHAPTER 4
AUDITIONS

The Importance of Agents

If you want to work as a music video dancer, you will have to attend countless auditions. Auditioning for a role is like interviewing for a job. You will want to do your best to convince the production team that you are right for the position.

If you choose to be a music video dancer in Los Angeles, one of the first auditions you might attend would be for an agent. Since there are so many dancers in Los Angeles going after the same jobs, agents have become a necessity. In many cases, you can't even audition for a job without one. A good agent or agency will provide assistance with developing a dancer's image and training. It is also the agent's responsibility to help you get auditions. Also, most dancers do not earn enough money from only dancing in music videos. They also audition for acting parts in movies and TV shows. This makes having an agent all the more important.

Headshots and Resumes

A headshot is a close-up picture of the dancer's face. A resume is a list of all your training and experience. They are often the first impressions you make to an agent, choreographer, or director. You need to have these with you at every audition you attend. In addition to a traditional headshot, you will need some full-body shots, too. Photographs are a good way for choreographers to get an idea of what your body looks like.

Resumes are usually your only chance to explain to people what kind of work and dance experience you have. Resumes should have a description of your physical features, training, and performance experience, along with your name and contact information. The resume must be laid out clearly on one page that fits on the back of your headshot.

Dressed for Success

Your audition clothes should flatter you, draw attention to your attractive features, and help you stand out in a room full of other talented dancers. Wear something that makes you feel good and will allow you to move easily. If you are comfortable with what you are wearing, it will show in your dancing. Many jazz and hip-hop dancers look for sporty street clothes and sneakers. Hats, bandanas, and bracelets are all popular accessories you can use to create your own statement.

Dancing at the Audition

You never know what a choreographer will ask you to do at an audition. If the audition

● Music video dancers understand that wearing the right clothes during a video shoot can be just as important as knowing all the dance moves.

is a large open call, you might learn a combination in a room with all of other dancers and perform it in smaller groups. If only a few dancers are being cast for individual roles, you might be auditioning by yourself, perhaps even on camera. You might be asked to freestyle or perform special skills.

Having a Good Attitude

A good attitude is very important during the audition process—and beyond. Even a simple thing like changing lines while learning a combination can tell choreographers whether he or she wants to hire you or not. Although a choreographer can help you improve your technique or coach you on performing his or her steps, your attitude is up to you. Walking in with a strong work ethic, professionalism, and respect for fellow dancers will be noticed.

Being respectful to your fellow dancers and coworkers is very important. It is a quality most choreographers want in their dancers. Choreographer Tina Landon notes, "If you're not going to trade lines with people when I ask you to...you're showing me you're just here for yourself. So, if you don't respect the needs of other dancers, you're not going to respect mine, either..."

31

Callbacks

Once an audition is held, some dancers may be "called back" for a second or more round of auditions. If you've been called back, it means you are still being considered for a part. At a callback audition, you may have to learn new material or repeat what you did at the first audition, so practicing at home is a good idea.

Dealing with Nerves

Just as in a live performance, nerves are a healthy part of every audition. While feeling nervous isn't much fun, it does not have to be viewed as a negative experience. Actually, the butterflies in your tummy are a sign that what you're doing really matters to you. If nerves are getting the better of you at auditions, you don't need to get rid of them. Just learn to manage them better.

● Auditions can be a nerve-wracking experience. Don't lose your cool. Remember, casting directors want to see you at your best.

Being nervous causes your body to make a lot of adrenaline. This might cause you to feel like you have even more energy than you do under normal circumstances. Most people develop physical outlets for their high energy level. Some people do a lot of pacing, talking, or biting their nails. Instead of releasing all that energy as nervous behavior, try channeling it toward your performance.

In the days before an audition, or while waiting for your turn at one, try to focus on doing your best with whatever lies ahead. When you are learning the combination, concentrate on the movement: Memorize it, get the movements into your body, and pay attention to what the choreographer says. When it is your turn to dance, give the combination everything you've got and have fun with it! If you go into every audition with a positive attitude, and your love of dance, your nerves will never get the best of you.

Handling Rejection

It is very important for you to remember that being rejected for a role is not a reflection of your worth as a person. Instead, it has to do with what the people producing the video feel they need. You might be the best dancer there, but if you are too tall or your schedule conflicts with the video's production schedule, you might not get the part. As long as you tried your best, you should consider it a successful audition, whether or not you get the job.

CHAPTER 5
YOUR BODY IS A TOOL

Staying Healthy

Being physically active takes a lot of strength and energy. Giving your body the nutrients and sleep it needs will keep you from getting tired. Many injuries happen because a body gets overworked and weak. It might be hard to eat right during a music video shoot, especially with all the free donuts, candy, and soda that are on most sets. However, try to choose yogurt, fruit, salads, vegetables, pastas, and sandwiches instead. Peanut butter or cheese sandwiches are good choices because they are packed with protein.

● Foods such as fruits and vegetables can help a music video dancer keep his or her energy up during long shoots.

During long shoots or intense rehearsals, caring for your body should be a top priority. Intense dancing during the shoots or rehearsals will cause you to sweat a lot. This will dehydrate you. It's very important that you drink at least eight glasses of water a day. Be prepared to change your clothing and shoes. This will help you to feel refreshed.

Physical Changes and Good Hygiene

Even now, as a student, you will probably notice that the harder you work, the more you sweat. To help yourself feel and smell fresh, keep some deodorant with you. Try a hot bath or shower to keep you feeling clean and relaxed. It will also soothe your tired and achy muscles after a long day of dancing.

As you grow older, you will see that your body is changing. These physical changes might affect your dance technique. Times of rapid growth and change mean that things you do in dance class may begin to feel different. Try not to get frustrated. These changes are all very natural and exciting aspects of your development as a dancer and a person.

Preventing Injuries

The stop-and-go action of shooting a music video presents special challenges to your body. When you stop moving and sit down, your muscles cool down. When they do, they literally get shorter and tighter. When you get up to perform again, your muscles won't be ready to work hard and fast. Resting on breaks is a good way of maintaining your energy level, but you must also keep your body warm by doing gentle stretches while you rest. A little extra care will prevent a lot of pulled muscles, strains, tears, and more severe injuries that may prevent you from dancing for a long time.

The Importance of Appearance

One reality of the music video dance business is its concentration on image, or how someone looks. Those in charge of the industry often have certain ideas about what is attractive or beautiful. On a job, you may be asked to wear clothing or makeup that you think may be inappropriate. If the producers are unwilling to consider any other options, you may find it is better for you not to continue the job. It

Music Video Jobs

If you decide that you do not want to be a music video dancer but still want to be a part of the process of making music videos, there are other careers in the field you can choose from:

Agent
Camera Operator
Casting Director
Choreographer
Costume or Set Designer
Film Editor
Hair and Makeup Designer
Lighting and Special Effects Designer
Sound Engineer
Video Director

may be difficult to turn down the chance to dance, but it is more important, in the long run, to maintain a healthy image of yourself—one that you like. People will be more willing to work with you in the future if they see you care for yourself and take pride in your own values.

exciting yet challenging career. With hard work, dedication, and a little luck, you just might find yourself dancing in some of the hottest music videos ever made!

A Career as a Music Video Dancer

Choosing a career is a big decision. You should talk about it with your parents and dance teachers to help you decide if this is the right career to you. Dancing in music videos is an

● If you work hard and master all the right moves, you might just find yourself before the cameras dancing with pop stars such as Annie Lennox (center), in a music video!

GLOSSARY

adrenaline (uh-**dren**-uh-lin) A chemical produced by your body when you are excited, frightened, or angry.

agent (**ay**-juhnt) Someone who arranges things for other people.

audition (aw-**dish**-uhn) A short performance by an actor, singer, musician, or dancer to see whether he or she is suitable for a part in a play, concert, etc.

barre (**bar**) The horizontal pole, usually made of wood, used as a handrail by ballet dancers to maintain balance as they exercise.

callback (**kawl**-bak) A second or additional audition for a theatrical part.

choreographer (kor-ee-**og**-ruh-fur) A person who creates ideas and movements for dancers.

dehydrate (dee-**hye**-drate) Not having enough water or other fluids that allow the body to function properly.

freestyle (free-**stile**) A way of dancing in which the dancer improvises, or creates, dance moves on the spot that reflect the music he or she is dancing to.

hygiene (**hye**-jeen) Actions taken by people to stay healthy and keep clean.

production (pruh-**duhk**-shuhn) Any form of entertainment that is presented to others.

resume (**re**-zuh-may) A brief list of all of the jobs, education, and awards a person has had.

shoot (**shoot**) To make a movie or video.

technique (tek-**neek**) A method or way of doing something that requires skill.

triple threat (**trip**-uhl **thret**) A performer who can dance, sing, and act.

vaudeville (**vaw**-de-vil) A stage show with various acts of song, dance, and comedy.

FOR MORE INFORMATION

Organizations

Millennium Dance Complex
5113 Lankershim Blvd.
North Hollywood, CA 91601
(818) 753-5081
Web site: http://www.morolandis.com/page1.htm

American Guild of Musical Artists
1430 Broadway, 14th floor
New York, NY 10018
(212) 265-3687
Web site: http://www.musicalartists.org/

Web Sites

Due to the changing nature of Internet links, the Rosen Publishing Group, Inc., has developed an online list of Web sites related to the subject of this book. This site is updated regularly. Please use this link to access the list:

http://www.rosenlinks.com/ccld/video/

FOR FURTHER READING

Books

Cefrey, Holly. *Backstage at a Music Video.* Danbury, CT: Children's Press, 2003.

Hughart, Jill (editor). *L. A. 411: Southern California's Professional Reference Guide for TV, Commercial and Music Video Production.* Los Angeles, CA: 411 Publishing, 2002.

Martins, Peter. *New York City Ballet Workout: Fifty Stretches and Exercises Anyone Can Do for a Strong, Graceful, and Sculpted Body.* New York: William Morrow & Company, 1997.

McGrath, Tom. *MTV: The Making of a Revolution.* Philadelphia, PA: Running Press Book Publishers, 1996.

Wolfram, Eric. *Your Dance Resume: A Preparatory Guide to the Audition.* San Francisco, CA: Dancepress, 1994.

Magazines and Publications

Curtain Call Dance Club Revue
P.O. Box 709
York, PA 17405-0709
Web site: http://www.cckids.com

Dance
333 7th Avenue, 11th floor
New York, NY 10001
(212) 979-4803
Web site: http://www.dancemagazine.com

Dancer
2829 Bird Avenue, Suite 5
PMB 231
Miami, FL 33133
(305) 460-3225
Web site: http://www.danceronline.com

Dance Spirit
Lifestyle Ventures, LLC
250 West 57th Street, Suite 420
New York, NY 10107
(212) 265-8890
Web site: http://www.dancespirit.com

BIBLIOGRAPHY

"Awards." Tina Landon Online. Retrieved June 2003 (http//www.tinalandononline.com/awards.shtml)

"Biography." Tina Landon Online. Retrieved June 2003 (http//www.tinalandononline.com/biography.shtml)

"Biography." Wonderful TJ Espinoza. Retrieved June 2003 (http://www.angelfire.com/co3/camlovestj/ biography.html)

Bloch, Allie. "Interview with TJ Espionza" PopZine Online. Retrieved June 2003 (http//www.popzineonline.com/tjespinoza.htm)

Cefrey, Holly. *Backstage at a Music Video*. Danbury, CT: Children's Press, 2003.

Dale, Grover. "Fresh Faces." Answers4dancers.com. Retrieved May 2003 (subscription service)

Dale, Grover. "Getting Started?" Answers4dancers.com. Retrieved May 2003 (subscription service)

Dale, Grover. "Music Video and Pop Tour Tips." Answers4dancers.com. Retrieved May 2003 (subscription service)

"Landon A Music Video Gig." Tina Landon Online. Retrieved June 2003 (http//www.tinalandononline.com /interviews/dancespirit_march2000.html)

McGrath, Tom. *MTV: The Making of a Revolution.* Philadelphia, PA: Running Press Book Publishers, 1996.

"Résumé." Tina Landon Online. Retrieved June 2003 (http//www.tinalandononline.com/resume.shtml)

"Toni Basil." VH1.com. Retrieved June 2003 (http//www.vh1.com/artists/az/basil_toni/bio.jhtml)

"Un–Dirty Dancing." Tina Landon Online. Retrieved June 2003 (http//www.tinalandononline.com/inter-views/controversy_aprilmay2000.html)

"Velvet Moves." Tina Landon Online. Retrieved June 2003 (http//www.tinalandononline.com/interviews/ vibe_online.html)

INDEX

About the Author

Originally from Ohio, Jenai Cutcher is a tap dancer, choreographer, teacher, and writer based in New York City.

Editor: Eric Fein **Book Design:** Christopher Logan and Erica Clendening

Developmental Editors: Nancy Allison, CMA, RME, and Susan Epstein